Ninja Foods

Recipes Included

CHRISTINA GLOWAC

Copyright © 2021 Christina Glowac
All rights reserved
First Edition

PAGE PUBLISHING
Conneaut Lake, PA

First originally published by Page Publishing 2021

ISBN 978-1-6624-4380-0 (pbk)
ISBN 978-1-6624-4382-4 (hc)
ISBN 978-1-6624-4381-7 (digital)

Printed in the United States of America

To my two Lyme ninjas, Trevor and Julie Anne.

Hi, my name is Trevor, and I am Julie Anne. Do you think you have what it takes to become a ninja with us? We are Lyme ninjas, and we need your help finding ninja foods. We have friends who are diabetes ninjas, cancer ninjas, gluten free ninjas, and other types of ninjas. What kind of ninja are you?

Ninja foods are foods that help heal our bodies. These are foods that are super healthy for us, like fruits and veggies. Lyme bugs hate ninja foods because it makes them weak. When you are a ninja, you need to help your body get stronger by staying away from foods like sugar and sweets, which can make your body feel worse.

Our goal is to eat all the ninja foods that we can every day so that we can get our bodies strong again. Before we get started, we need to see your ninja moves! Get your ninja mask on, and let's get started.

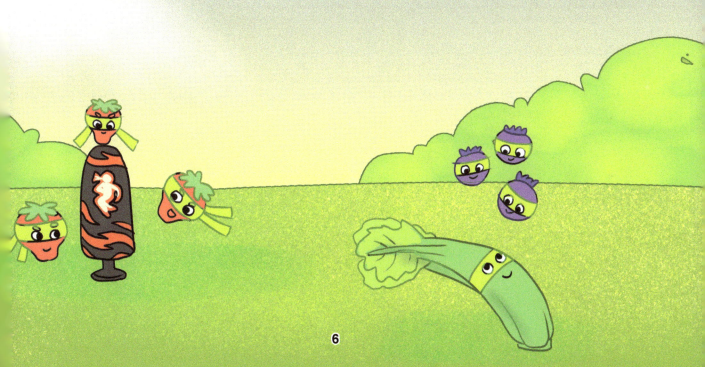

Show us how you zap, zip, boom, iyay! Wow, you are really good at that. We think you might be ready.

Point to all the foods that are ninja foods. Make sure you yell *zap, zip, boom* and *iyay* for every ninja food that you find.

Ninjas, ready and go!

How did you do? Did you find all the ninja foods?

By eating our ninja foods, we are helping to heal our bodies.

You are such a great ninja! It's your job to help others know the ninja foods you should be eating to help your body.

There are lots of other ninjas out there who are working hard to heal their bodies as well.

Keep up the great work and keep eating all your ninja foods!

Ninja Food Recipes

We have added some of our favorite ninja food recipes so you can still have treats like cakes, ice cream, popsicles, and brownies. The secret is that we make them with our ninja foods. You can help make these treats.
(Please consult with your doctor if your child has dietary restrictions.)

Ninja Banana Ice Cream

Freeze a bunch of bananas without the peels. Pull some out of the freezer, and let them sit on the counter so they start to defrost (or you can pop them in the microwave). Put the bananas into a blender and blend until smooth. It comes out as creamy as real ice cream. You can add frozen mango as well or fresh strawberries. You can also add in some cocoa powder to make it chocolate banana ice cream.

Farmers Market

This is one of our go-to favorites in our house. We play "farmers market," and put together snack plates of what you might find at your local farmers market: fruits, cheeses, olives, and meats. It is so yummy and feels like a fancy appetizer. My kids love anything that I let them eat with toothpicks. We actually have little ninja sword toothpicks that they use.

Ninja Chocolate Banana Brownies, Cupcakes, or Cake

Ingredients

3/4 cup almond flour, or your favorite gluten-free flour
1/4 teaspoon salt
1/2 teaspoon baking soda
4 large eggs (I usually use 2 eggs and 2/3 cup of unsweetened applesauce)

1/4 cup oil
1/4 cup honey
2 medium-sized ripe bananas, mashed (about 1 cup)
1 teaspoon vanilla extract
1/2 cup of cocoa powder, if you want to make them chocolate

Instructions

1. Preheat oven to 350 degrees.
2. Mix all the wet ingredients together, including the mashed-up bananas.
3. Mix together the dry ingredients. Slowly add the dry ingredients to the wet ingredients.
4. Pour into a greased pan. You can either make cupcakes, cake, or pour batter into a large rectangle baking dish to make brownies.
5. Bake at 350 degrees until a toothpick inserted in the center comes out clean. Cooking time varies, depending on what you decide to make and if you are doubling the recipe. Cooking time ranges from thirty minutes to an hour.
6. After they cool, I always put individual portion sizes into zip lock snack bags and then I freeze them. In the morning, I put a frozen treat into Trevor's lunchbox, and it is defrosted by snack time. This is also the recipe we use for his birthday parties, and his friends always *love* them.

Ninja Baked Apples

Ingredients

4 apples
1 cup rolled oats
1/8 cup of maple syrup
1 teaspoon ground cinnamon
1/4 cup of butter or ghee, melted

Instructions

1. Preheat oven to 350 degrees.
2. Core out the apples, making a large well in the center. You can either buy an apple baker, or you can arrange apples in a baking dish.
3. Mix oats, maple syrup, and cinnamon together in a bowl.
4. Then add in the butter.
5. Fill the apples with the oatmeal filling.
6. Bake in the preheated oven until apples are tender and the filling is bubbling, about thirty minutes.
7. You can also core out an apple, add some butter, a little maple syrup and a sprinkle of cinnamon, and put it into the microwave for two to three minutes.
8. This is Julie Anne's favorite dessert.

Ninja Popsicles

Get some popsicles molds. Have your kids mash up their favorite fruits, and scoop them into the molds. You can do just one flavor (i.e., banana), or you can layer the fruits to make the pops more colorful. Put in the freezer overnight, and your kids now have popsicles that are safe to eat.

Ninja Pumpkin Bread, Muffins, or Cake

Ingredients

2 cups of flour (I usually use 1 cup of almond flour and 1 cup of gluten-free flour)
1/2 teaspoon salt
1 teaspoon baking soda
1/2 teaspoon baking powder
1 teaspoon cloves
1 teaspoon cinnamon
1 teaspoon nutmeg
3/4 cup of softened butter
3/4 cup of honey
1/3 cup of unsweetened applesauce
2 eggs
1 can of pumpkin

Instructions

1. Preheat oven to 350 degrees.
2. Mix together all your wet ingredients.
3. Mix together your dry ingredients. Slowly add the dry ingredients to the wet ingredients.
4. Pour into a greased pan. You can either make cupcakes, cake, or pour batter into a large rectangle baking dish.
5. Bake at 350 degrees until a toothpick inserted in the center comes out clean. Cooking time varies depending on what you decide to make and if you are doubling the recipe. Cooking time ranges from thirty minutes to an hour.
6. After they cool, freeze individual servings as explained under the Ninja Chocolate Banana Brownies recipe.

Ninja Apple Bake

Ingredients

3/4 cup brown rice flour
3/4 teaspoon baking powder
Pinch salt
3 tablespoons melted ghee or butter
3 Macintosh apples

2 flax eggs (2 tablespoons of ground flax seed mixed with 5 tablespoons of water)
3/4 cup unsweetened applesauce
1 teaspoon vanilla

Instructions

1. Preheat oven to 400 degrees.
2. Combine all the wet ingredients. For the flax eggs, stir to combine flax and water, then let it sit for a few minutes so it thickens up. Add applesauce, ghee/butter, and vanilla.
3. Add in the baking powder, salt, and brown rice flour. Stir everything to combine.
4. Dice up apples. You can peel them or keep the skin on. Stir apples into mix.
5. Spread out mixture in a greased baking dish. Cook at 400 degrees for 50 minutes to an hour. It tends to remain a bit gooey in the center. We usually double the recipe so we have leftovers for the next day.

Ninja Chocolate Chip Cookies

Ingredients

2 cups almond flour (or 1 cup almond flour and 1 cup gluten free flour)
1/4 teaspoon salt
1/2 teaspoon baking soda
1/4 cup melted butter
1/4 cup maple syrup
2 teaspoons vanilla
1/2 cup chocolate chips (we use Lily's Milk Chocolate Baking Chips)

Instructions

1. Preheat oven to 350 degrees.
2. Combine all wet ingredients. Butter, syrup and vanilla.
3. Add in dry ingredients. Flour, salt and baking soda.
4. Stir in chocolate chips.
5. Roll into balls and place on a greased cookie sheet.
6. Take a fork and press down the cookie balls so they are flat. I go in two directions so it makes a design.
7. Bake at 350 degrees for 15-20 minutes. If you make smaller cookies, it will take 15 minutes, if you make larger cookies, it will take 20 minutes.
8. Here is an example of our ninja recipes packed up in snack bags. I put them into the freezer and then Trevor can grab the snack he wants to bring to school.

About the Author

Christina B. Glowac, MSW, LICSW, brings her own family's personal experience with Lyme disease, as well as her background as a social worker, together to write this engaging book to support children and families in dealing with the dietary restrictions that occur as a result of illness. The lifestyle changes and treatments that she and her children have gone through have been significant, and her desire to write this book comes from a place deep in her heart. Her hope is that this book can help other parents ease the difficulty of the healing process that unfolds when children get sick. Ninja foods was a key concept in her house to help her son deal with the dietary changes that he had to face.

Christina lives in Vermont, with her family. She loves spending time with them, skiing at the mountain, being by the ocean, and playing with her dog. Follow Christina on Instagram at Ninjafoods_childrensbook and on her Facebook page: Ninja Foods.

We left some space at the end so you can add some of your favorite Ninja Foods Recipes to this book. You can share your recipe ideas with us on our Facebook page Ninja Foods. We would also love to see photos of you making some of our recipes and reading our book.

CPSIA information can be obtained
at www.ICGtesting.com
Printed in the USA
BVHW020707160222
629158BV00002B/20